GEMINI

HOROSCOPE

2024

Alina A. Rubi

Angeline Rubi

Published Independently

Who is Gemini?

Dates: *May 21st - June 21st*

Day: *Wednesday*

Color: *Blue*

Element: *Air*

Compatibility: *Libra, Aries, and Aquarius*

Symbol: Ⅱ

Mode: *Mutable*

Polarity: *Male*

Ruling planet: *Mercury*

House: *3*

Metal: *Mercury*

Quartz: *Crystal, beryl, and topaz.*

Constellation: *Gemini*

Gemini Personality

Gemini has a great adaptability and versatility, they are intellectual, eloquent, affectionate, and intelligent. They have a lot of energy and vitality, they love to talk, to read, to do several things at the same time.

This is a sign that enjoys the unusual and novelty, the more variety in their life, the better. His character is dual and complex, sometimes contradictory. On the one hand, he is versatile, but on the other hand, he can be dishonest.

Gemini is the sign of twins and, as such, their character and way of being is dual. They represent contradiction and change their mind or mood easily.

Gemini are very active and need to be always busy, they love to multitask and try new challenges.

They have the happiness, imagination, creativity, and restlessness of children. Some start new activities and challenges with enthusiasm, but often lack the constancy to finish them. From their point of view life is a game and they look for fun and new experiences. Gemini is the most childlike sign of the zodiac.

Their good humor and communicative ability disappear when faced with a problem, as they tend to become discouraged in the worst circumstances and leave it to others to find solutions.

Gemini are very intelligent, they ask everything. This makes them masters of debate. They are among the signs with the highest IQ.

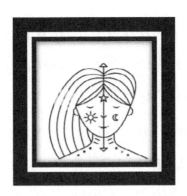

General Horoscope for Gemini

This will be an excellent year for Gemini. Jupiter, the planet of luck and opportunity, moves into your sign on May 25, and this only happens once every 12 years.

During this transit of Jupiter showers of opportunities will come into your life and you will feel more optimistic. This is a new beginning, a new path, a new journey.

The year 2024 will bring you wonderful luck, you will be inspired to do something new or accomplish something you have been meaning to do for many years.

Luck and your efforts will establish your name in your professional area, and you will create a new identity in business. In addition, you will be able to complete an old business or project that has been stalled for the past year.

You will earn a lot of money, but to get it you must avoid making hasty decisions and the desire to build an empire overnight.

If you are employed, you will work harder than last year, but this will give you new opportunities and even offers in new companies. In general, Jupiter will make sure you get the best opportunities.

After the month of July, you should concentrate, as Saturn retrograde can create some challenging and tense situations for you. During this period, you will have to proceed with caution, and plan carefully to avoid mistakes.

During 2024 you will be very happy and satisfied with your partner most of the time. There will be some conflicts and misunderstandings in your relationship after the second half of the year, and it will also be a period when marriage prospects will not materialize.

Give your partner priority, you must make every effort.

If you are single, you will meet someone, the possibilities are stronger after May. You may meet your future partner during a trip, you will create a bond over time that will develop into a deep friendship, eventually turning it into a sentimental relationship.

Two eclipses will occur in your area of love, a Lunar eclipse on March 25 and a solar eclipse on October 2.

The Lunar eclipse will make you feel closer to loved ones with whom you have a healthy connection, and you will move away from anyone who is toxic. This can be the perfect time to work on pending love issues.

The solar eclipse can bring a new love into your life. If you are single, you will be motivated to go out and attract attention, while if you are in a relationship, you will add sparks of passion.

Your financial health will improve in 2024 and you will benefit from new sources of income. You may receive additional income from commissions, stock market, bank interest or who knows if the lottery.

If you have dreamed of buying a house or a new car, it will come true this year, and if you need a loan, you will get it easily. If you work hard professionally, your bank account will increase.

You may move or fix up your home, and this change may bring setbacks in the family. You must have patience to overcome these problems so that happiness can return to your family life.

You will maintain good health throughout the year, but there may be some minor problems in the middle of the year as you will feel depressed and tired due to stress. This may manifest with digestive problems due to lack of appetite and restlessness caused by setbacks.

Love

This year can bring emotional ups and downs, you must remember that it is normal to experience a variety of emotions and have mood swings from time to time. To cope with your emotions, it is important that you find healthy ways to cope, such as talking to a trusted friend or family member, practicing relaxation techniques such as meditation, or seeking the support of a mental therapist if necessary. You should take care of yourself and seek support if needed.

This year is excellent for those Gemini who are looking to establish a relationship. If you have thought about getting engaged, this is the perfect year to do so. You will make progress in your love life this year.

Although you will be very romantic and dreamy during this year, and you will tend to idealize the person you love, you must be careful because your fantasies may not be totally in accordance with reality and that will lead you to suffer disappointments in the future.

Try to be coherent, realistic, and accept the other person as he or she is. Love during this year will tend to be platonic.

In any case, this year will be very favorable for coexistence and for all types of association.

Economy

This year will be great for you in the economic area. You will achieve your goal of changing jobs, and this new beginning will bring you many opportunities.

Your courage will be admired by others, but it is important to choose your battles wisely, as standing up for what you believe in can sometimes have negative consequences.

The planets will give you the green light in money matters. Mercury, your ruling planet, will fully support you and make sure you have your bank accounts full of money.

In May, Jupiter transits into your sign, which will have a beneficial effect on your finances and career, as well as your relationships.

Your financial resources will grow, and it will be a good year for long-term investments.

Of course, all this will not come to you without effort, you will have to work, be disciplined, and continue to try during the year.

Jupiter will favor the establishment of new connections with important people and the strengthening of your social ties.

Gemini Health

You must make a conscious effort to prioritize your physical health, remembering that good health is a key component to success in all areas of your life. You should plan to lose extra weight and incorporate regular exercise, especially outdoor activities.

The way you eat is important, so you should pay attention to your diet, increasing protein intake and limiting carbohydrates so that you can avoid weight gain and digestive problems.

Some Gemini will probably feel tired as their immune system will be weak. You will have stages of low energy levels, but that will improve, and you will regain your vigor.

If you have any chronic health problems, such as diabetes or blood pressure, you should be careful throughout the year. Don't forget that wellness starts at home. Encouraging you to eliminate unhealthy foods from your kitchen and try to stock up on organic foods. This is a good time to start preparing your meals at home instead of buying processed foods. If you start eating this way you will feel better and better.

Family

You will be more emotionally involved with those you consider family. You want your home to be a sanctuary, a safe space, and you will strive to eliminate problems in a healthy way.

During periods of Mercury retrograde in your home you may break some household appliances or have some problems with water. This can not only be annoying, but it will bring family disputes and most likely you will pay the blame. Be patient because those appliances will most likely need routine maintenance.

Many of your close family members will be asking you for advice frequently during this year and that will make you feel indispensable.

Some sentimental changes will take place in your family nucleus. Perhaps your children or siblings will introduce you to their new partners and this will give a new dynamic to your family. These will be beneficial changes.

You will get back in touch with people you were distanced from, you will give them second chances and you will realize that not everything is what it seems.

Important Dates

- *May 20- Sun enters Gemini.*

- *May 23- Venus enters Gemini.*

- *May 25 the planet Jupiter enters your sign. It begins a period of much action, of new perspectives, of goals that can be fulfilled.*

- *June 03- Mercury enters Gemini.*

- *June 6 New Moon in your sign. More opportunities come your way, be sure to make the most of them.*

- *July 20 the planet Mars transits into your sign until September 4. Mars in your sign will fill you with energy and enthusiasm so that you can accomplish all your goals and objectives. It is a perfect time for new beginnings.*

- *December 15 Full Moon in your sign. This will be the time when you will get the results of everything you have done so far.*

Gemini Monthly Horoscopes 2024

January 2024

This month, it is advisable that you control your anger and ego and think twice before saying something to someone.

You should seek advice before making important decisions regarding any investment. Avoid planning any travel or spending on expensive items. This is a favorable period for dealing with legal matters.

You will overcome any professional obstacles, but it is important that you make decisions after seeking advice from experts. Your efforts will lead you to a favorable position in your workplace, and you may have opportunities for a job change with attractive offers from successful companies.

You must be very careful with disputes and misunderstandings, as your ego can lead to problems in your relationships.

If you are single, you will meet someone special.

Prioritize regular health check-ups, avoid junk and fatty foods.

At the end of the month, you will have to put a lot of effort into whatever work you do, but you will get the results according to your expectations. Hard work will be rewarded, and you will earn enough money to help you through difficult times. Family life will be good. There will be harmony among all family members.

Lucky numbers

13 - 15 - 17 - 20 - 28

February 2024

This month you will face a lot of stress as many obligations will accumulate and you will be involved in an agitation in which you will not be able to enjoy anything. It is important that you do not get mixed up in mentally demanding projects, and that you plan some weekends where you can be in contact with friends and nature. You should also spend some periods alone so that you can free your mind and put your priorities in order.

If you have become attached to someone very special, this is the ideal month to take the first step, as you will be very seductive and eloquent to that potential partner. There is the potential for a stable relationship.

Be careful with your health, perhaps you overindulged in eating at the end of last year and now the results of your carelessness are beginning to show. Stressful situations within your family circle may also cause your health to weaken.

If you are married or in a firm relationship, a separation may occur because of a long trip your partner will be taking.

Lucky numbers

4 - 18 - 25 - 35 - 36

March 2024

This month you will concentrate on planning and making important decisions as you will have very clear priorities. Try to focus on your goals and plan how you will accomplish them. Patience will become your fulcrum.

Although it seems that you have everything clear and that nothing bothers you, you may experience states of depression during this month, be very careful. You must realize that it is not necessary to live fast, nor is it necessary to dedicate yourself exclusively to work. Evenings this month are perfect for reading books or watching movies in the company of your friends or partner.

Try to increase your social life and meet new people to establish new bonds of friendship, you must overcome loneliness. Fate will put in front of you people who will play an important role in your future. You will probably initiate important professional relationships, and you will probably establish deep sentimental ties. If you are single, you are likely to start a relationship that will be formalized as a marriage in the future.

Expect problems, with older people. This is not the time to make repairs in your home.

Lucky numbers
10 - 18 - 25 - 34 - 35

April 2024

This month you will come out of your bubble and shine among other people thanks to your sense of humor. You will have quick reactions, which will dazzle not only your work colleagues, but also your bosses. Establishing new contacts will not be a problem for you and you will make many business trips.

If you practice physical exercises, you will be prone to muscle problems. Although sports will serve to relax you from the whirlwind of thoughts about your work, charging you with new energy.

If you've been thinking about starting a new hobby, this month's energy is good for any creative activity, whether it's painting, writing, or creating music.

You will also be successful in your studies, so it would be a good idea to take a class related to your profession or the technological field.

Your economic wounds begin to heal because Jupiter is approaching your sign, keep discipline and moderation.

Lucky numbers
5 - 10 - 11 - 22 - 26

May 2024

This month you will feel the need to be in contact with your close friends. You will long for a hug, the closeness and security of those who love you. Remember to grow your self-esteem.

May is a month full of emotions thanks to the transit of Jupiter through your sign, thanks to this influence your ability to produce money will increase, but it is advisable to balance the rhythm of your life, and to rest, so that you can take advantage of the opportunities with tranquility.

This is the perfect time to take stock of your strengths and weaknesses. Even if you have plans for expansion and diversification, remember that the only way to move forward is to know where you are and what you have.

Enjoying your body is important to have a healthy balance, for that reason as soon as the sun rises, before fulfilling your obligations, try to have contact with objects that seduce all your senses.

Improve your respiratory tract by placing essential oils under your pillow, avoid drafts and avoid being barefoot.

Lucky numbers
5 - 7 - 8 - 19 - 27

June 2024

This month your cooking skills will be highlighted, and you will start experimenting with different healthy food recipes.

Before getting involved in a dispute, think about whether it is worth it. Words have the power to heal, but they can also hurt. You may regret your arrogant comments in the future.

If you don't have a partner, you may be wondering if you should say yes to that request that a person has made to you on social networks. You should do it because that person is going to be very special in your life, and it will mean a love story.

You must avoid staying awake at night, lack of rest is harmful. Organize your schedule better so that the necessary sleep time is not affected.

If you have a partner, you may have forbidden loves or secret relationships that will complicate your well-being. Do not complicate yourself with relationships that do not represent your true ideal.

If you want to start your own business, the end of the month is ideal for financing options.

Revelations in love, it is very possible that you find out something that your partner had told you.

Lucky numbers
6 - 7 - 12 - 17 - 25

July 2024

A month full of love and blessings. You will be brimming with good humor, and great ideas. If you do not have a partner, let your intuition play a great role in your actions this month.

Also take advantage and go in search of new knowledge, such as reading, listening to self-help audios where you learn meditation techniques that will help you in all areas of your life.

Family relationships will also flourish, and you will communicate with even your most distant family. You will be amazed at how much fun you will have together with them.

It is likely that at work you will find out about some gossip that involves you, but that is no reason to close the doors to personal relationships where you work. You just must be very careful about telling your personal life.

You must also learn to practice deafness and turn a deaf ear to those conversations full of negativity and hate that insist on underestimating your efforts.

Lucky numbers
4 - 11 - 12 - 20 - 28

August 2024

This month you will want to spend time with your children, and your family in general. Perhaps you will go on vacation together to a tropical place. Everyone will be very cheerful, and you will have a lot of fun. If you don't have children, then take advantage of this mood, and share with your friends' children, who will undoubtedly thank you for it.

If you and your partner are planning to have children, this month is ideal. During this stage you will be sociable and a love for animals will be born. It is likely that you will decide to go to the animal shelter and decide to adopt one as a pet.

At work there will be a strong atmosphere of tension and uncertainty that can put you headlong on the brink of an emotional upheaval. If you happen to be unhappy at work, start looking for a better one. Remember that your mental health is valuable.

Do not despair, as you have managed to emerge triumphant from worse scenarios.

A good exercise for your mind is to meditate. You need to go deep within yourself to find that peace that you think is lost but is hidden within your heart. Everything you need has always been within you.

Lucky numbers
3 - 7 - 17 - 22 - 25

September 2024

This month you will long to be alone and at peace because you want to focus on yourself. You have many unresolved questions that need to be answered, and this period is perfect for that. Nature is very important so don't stay at home. Thanks to that you will be able to enjoy excellent mental and physical health, but don't forget that having the advice of people who love you could get you out of any crisis.

There are urgent things that need to be solved in the short term, but you are finding it difficult to give them the right solution, focus on solving all these problems so you can continue moving forward in your life. The worst thing is to have something pending unresolved.

A well-known businessperson is going to look for you to offer you to do business, you should pay close attention because it is a very good opportunity.

Try not to carry the worries and stress of work into all areas of your life because this could throw you off balance.

At the end of the month your cold will give reason to talk and arouse malicious comments around you.

Lucky numbers
2 - 10 - 19 - 25 - 36

October 2024

During the month of October, you will want to change the atmosphere of your home and you will be very excited about renovating it. First you will do a deep cleaning that you have been planning for a long time.

In your relationship you will find yourself in a situation that will make you very jealous, you will feel threatened, and you will start to fight. However, this reaction is very harmful, so analyze the situation well, so that with a clear mind you can avoid acting on impulse. Besides, things will not be as serious as they seem. Your health may be a little weak if you do not respect your rest hours and the way you nourish yourself. At work you will have some disappointments because you thought you could trust your work colleagues, but a particular situation will show you how wrong you were. Your way of being and your knowledge have aroused the envy of those around you and so they will try a betrayal. It's good to know who you work with. Don't start arguments. Take your time to calmly plan a good strategy to vindicate yourself.

Lucky numbers
1 - 9 - 11 - 17 - 26

November 2024

You will be a bit introverted this month, and for that reason your friends will push you aside. You will be focused on doing many things that are your priorities.

Your sixth sense will be sharpened, and this will help you to see the dark intentions of people, avoiding deception.

An emotional problem with someone in your family could make you want to run away and disappear. Don't fight your impulses. That's probably just what you need to clear your head and be able to deal with that family member.

A very special person is going to catch your attention, a person who has always been a mystery to you.

You must give yourself the opportunity for this mystery to manifest, don't go and make any interference. Don't forget that the process is always much more important than the result. You must trust your intuition because you will experience an extremely romantic adventure.

If you like swimming, running or yoga, why not do them all? You have a lot of energy and it's good to channel it.

Lucky numbers

10 - 11 - 23 - 26 - 35

December 2024

Last month of the year, one in which you will go crazy with love and happy with so many blessings you will receive. You are going to meet a person who will revolutionize your hormones, and those who have a partner should be very careful because they will be tempted to be unfaithful. You may be wondering if you are happy in your current relationship, you need to answer this question.

There will be a lot going on in your work and personal life, so learn to calm down. One way to do this is by writing, doing exercises, or studying.

Your leadership potential will be emphasized and will expand to all areas of your life, which is why you must control your temperament.

Don't leave things unfinished for next year if you must finish something you started a few months ago you should start finishing it, whether it is a project or a problem you must solve.

Plan well all the things you have next year 2025, and most importantly: do not give the opportunity to return to a person who hurt you.

Lucky numbers
5 - 12 - 22 - 25 - 27

The Tarot Cards, an Enigmatic and Psychological World.

The word Tarot means "royal road", it is a millenary practice, it is not known exactly who invented card games in general, nor the Tarot in particular; there are the most dissimilar hypotheses in this sense.

Some say that it arose in Atlantis or Egypt, but others believe that tarots came from China or India, from the ancient land of the gypsies, or that they arrived in Europe through the Cathars. The fact is that tarot cards distill astrological, alchemical, esoteric, and religious symbolism, both Christian and pagan.

Until recently, if you mentioned the word 'tarot' to some people, it was common for them to imagine a gypsy sitting in front of a crystal ball in a room surrounded by mysticism, or to think of black magic or witchcraft, but nowadays this has changed.

This ancient technique has been adapting to the new times, it has joined technology and many young people feel a deep interest in it.

Young people have isolated themselves from religion because they believe that they will not find the solution to what they need there, they realized the duality of this, something that does not happen with spirituality. All over the social networks you find accounts dedicated to the study and tarot readings, since everything related to esotericism is fashionable, in fact, some hierarchical decisions are made considering the tarot or astrology.

What is remarkable is that the predictions that are usually related to tarot are not the most sought after, the ones related to self-knowledge and spiritual counseling are the most requested.

The tarot is an oracle, through its drawings and colors, we stimulate our psychic sphere, the innermost part that goes beyond the natural. Many people turn to the tarot as a spiritual or psychological guide because we live in uncertain times, and this pushes us to seek answers in spirituality.

It is such a powerful tool that tells you concretely what is going on in your subconscious so that you can perceive it through the lens of a new wisdom.

Carl Gustav Jung, the famed psychologist, used the symbols of tarot cards in his psychological studies.

He created the theory of archetypes, where he discovered an extensive sum of images that help in analytical psychology.

The use of drawings and symbols to appeal to a deeper understanding is frequently used in psychoanalysis. These allegories are part of us, corresponding to symbols of our subconscious and our mind.

Our unconscious has dark areas, and when we use visual techniques, we can reach different parts of it and reveal elements of our personality that we do not know. When you can decode these messages through the pictorial language of tarot, you can choose what decisions to make in life to create the destiny you really want.

The tarot with its symbols teaches us that a different universe exists, especially nowadays where everything is so chaotic, and a logical explanation is sought for everything.

Death, Tarot Card for Gemini 2024

New beginnings. Openings and changes. You will start a new life with a different style.

The sadness is left behind, the happy and peaceful days begin now in 2024.

It represents the change of a belief pattern, of a lifestyle. It symbolizes the end of a cycle or a change through pain.

It symbolizes everything that ends and forces us to move to a different plane of existence. This card allows to change the present elements to a more sublime state.

You may find that your options are being restricted at every step you take. The best course of action lies in the one thing you can control: Face this situation with patience and be ready to move when the situation changes.

Avoid stress and negative emotions whenever they arise.

You should take situations more calmly, sometimes it is better to keep your head down and keep quiet to avoid unnecessary conflicts over unimportant matters.

Runes of the Year 2024

Runes are a set of symbols that form an alphabet. "Rune" means secret and symbolizes the noise of one stone colliding with another. Runes are a legendary visionary and magical method.

Runes do not serve for exact predictions, but they do serve to guide you about a future event, an issue, or a decision. Runes have a specific meaning for the person who wants it, but also some message related to the adversities that arise in life.

SOWELU, Gemini Rune 2024

The time has come to expose certain secrets of your life. This Rune forces you to admit things that you have been determined to hide.

This year 2024 is the year to act, renew and transform yourself so that you can have abundance. To achieve this, it is important that you are open to possibilities, and that you analyze everything from various perspectives.

It is advisable to remove yourself from all situations and people that cause you stress. You must stop being proud, humility is important when facing limitations. Do not be conceited, even if you are virtuous.

This rune makes things easier for you because of its power to illuminate the way. It helps you to reason and to draw a clear map to follow, to achieve your goals.

If you have stalled plans or projects, it's time to fight to move them forward. Sowelu gives you the impulse and tells you that it is time to act. Sowelu advises you to be clear about your intentions.

This rune represents the fire that illuminates our path and the decisions we make.

Lucky Colors

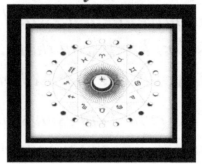

Colors affect us psychologically; they influence our appreciation of things, opinion about something or someone, and can be used to influence our decisions.

Traditions to welcome the new year vary from country to country, and on the night of December 31 we take stock of all the positive and negative things we experienced in the year that is leaving. We start thinking about what to do to transform our luck in the new year ahead.

There are several ways to attract positive energies towards us when we receive the new year, and one of them is to wear or wear accessories of a specific color that attracts what we wish for the year to begin.

Colors have energetic charges that influence our lives, so it is always advisable to receive the year dressed in a color that attracts the energies of what we want to achieve.

For that there are colors that vibrate positively with each zodiac sign, so the recommendation is that you wear the clothes with the hue that will make you attract prosperity, health, and love in 2024. (These colors can also be used during the rest of the year for important occasions, or to enhance your days).

Remember that, although the most common is to wear red underwear for passion, pink for love and yellow or gold for abundance, it is never too much to include in our attire the color that most benefits our zodiac sign.

Gemini

Yellow.

Yellow keywords: *Happiness, joy, intelligence, innovation, energy, strength, and power.*

Yellow will bring you happiness because it is a bright, cheerful color that symbolizes luxury and how to be festive every day.

It is associated with the intellectual part of the mind and the expression of our thoughts.

When you use this color you will get an extra touch of energy, warmth, and a youthful countenance. This warm color will attract the attention of anyone who is next to you and will fill the spaces where you are present with energy.

Yellow benefits concentration and memory.

Lucky Charms

Who doesn't own a lucky ring, a chain that never comes off, or an object that they wouldn't give away for anything in the world? We all attribute a special power to certain items that belong to us and this special character that they assume for us makes them magical objects. For a talisman to act and influence circumstances, its wearer must have faith in it, and this will transform it into a prodigious object, able to fulfill everything that is asked of it.

In the everyday sense an amulet is any object that propitiates good as a preventive measure against evil, harm, disease, and witchcraft.

Amulets for good luck can help you to have a year 2024 full of blessings in your home, work, with your family, attract money and health. For the amulets to work properly you should not lend them to anyone else, and you should always have them at hand.

Amulets have existed in all cultures and are made from elements of nature that serve as catalysts of energies that help create human desires.

The amulet is assigned the power to ward off evils, spells, diseases, disasters or to counteract evil wishes cast through the eyes of others.

Amulet for Gemini

Archangel Michael.

The archangel Michael is the most famous of the archangels. He is the most invoked and the one most people ask for help. All this is because he is a spiritual warrior. You should use an image of St. Michael to invoke his blessings and to grant you strength and protection from evil forces.

This archangel will also help you find your life's purpose. Invoking him when you need help will give you the courage and determination you need. When you evoke him in times of distress, he helps you regain your calm.

When you call on him, he will intervene and fight for you so that you can get rid of the negativity.

Lucky Quartz

We are all attracted to diamonds, rubies, emeralds and sapphires, obviously precious stones. Semi-precious stones such as carnelian, tiger's eye, white quartz, and lapis lazuli are also highly prized as they have been used as ornaments and symbols of power for thousands of years.

What many do not know is that they were valued for more than their beauty: each had a sacred significance, and their healing properties were as important as their ornamental value.

Crystals still have the same properties in our days, most people are familiar with the most popular ones such as amethyst, malachite and obsidian, but nowadays there are new crystals such as larimar, petalite and phenacite that have become known.

A crystal is a solid body with a geometrically regular shape, crystals were formed when the earth was created and have continued to metamorphose as the planet has changed, crystals are the DNA of the earth, they are miniature stores that contain the development of our planet over millions of years.

Some have been subjected to enormous pressures and others grew in chambers buried deep underground, others dripped into being. Whatever form they take, their crystalline structure can absorb, conserve, focus and emit energy. At the heart of the crystal is the atom, its electrons, and protons. The atom is dynamic and is composed of a series of particles that rotate around the center in constant motion, so that, although the crystal may seem motionless, it is a living molecular mass that vibrates at a certain frequency, and this is what gives the crystal its energy.

Gems used to be a royal and priestly prerogative, the priests of Judaism wore a plaque on their chest full of precious stones which was much more than an emblem to designate their function, as it transferred power to the wearer.

Men have worn stones since the stone age as they had a protective function guarding their wearers from various evils. Today's crystals have the same power, and we can select our jewelry not only according to their external attractiveness, having them near us can boost our energy (orange carnelian), clean the space around us (amber) or attract wealth (citrine).

Certain crystals such as smoky quartz and black tourmaline could absorb negativity, emitting a pure and clean energy.

Wearing a black tourmaline around your neck protects you from electromagnetic emanations including from cell phones, a citrine will not only attract wealth, but also help you keep it, place it in the wealth part of your home (the back left corner furthest away from the front door). If you are looking for love, crystals can help you, place a rose quartz in the relationship corner of your home (the back right corner furthest from the front door) its effect is so powerful that you may want to add an amethyst to offset the attraction.

You can also use rhodochrosite, love will come your way.

Crystals can heal and give balance, some crystals contain minerals known for their therapeutic properties, malachite has a high concentration of copper, wearing a malachite bracelet allows the body to absorb minimal amounts of copper.

Lapis lazuli relieves migraine, but if the headache is caused by stress, amethyst, amber or turquoise placed above the eyebrows will relieve it.

Quartz and minerals are jewels of mother earth, give yourself the opportunity, and connect with the magic they give off.

Lucky Quartz for Gemini

White quartz or rock crystal.

An energy receiver par excellence, and amplifier of positive vibrations at all levels. It helps with mental concentration and reinforces or enhances the other quartz. It is the most used therapeutically.

It symbolizes happiness and is sometimes used to honor a birth or to offer peace after death. Its main function is to bring balance and peace by mobilizing or deactivating energies.

It will help you resist bad moments, negative thoughts such as guilt, or emotional problems. It also protects you from fears and anxieties. Its healing properties improve cognition and enhance mental agility. It helps to make memory faster and to learn as it increases knowledge and the faculty of listening.

With this crystal, you will become patient.

Gemini and Zodiac Sign Compatibility

Gemini is an air sign that can get along without problems among friends, parties, and nights out. Gemini is ruled by Mercury, the planet of communication, so you can always find interesting topics for conversation.

Gemini is an excellent anecdotist, and his dynamic energy and magnetism attract romantic partners. Jealous people should know that Gemini is never alone, as he always has fans and followers. Because Gemini expresses his emotions outwardly, he loves to converse. This self-expression is paramount to the Mercurial twin, so he needs all lines of communication to be open, and willing to receive information, to his Geminian.

He doesn't care how his ideas are conveyed, the action of sharing his thoughts is more important than what he says. There is nothing Gemini despises more than leisure; he is always busy. He is always on the go with his many entertainments, inclinations, and social obligations.
This air sign may complain about being overworked, but when you analyze their daily schedule all their errands are optional, which shows that Gemini's schedule is nothing more than the result of their unique duality.
Gemini loves to share their thoughts and ideas, but they are not good listeners and are easily distracted,

so it is key that you make sure your Gemini partner pays attention to you.

If by chance you see that he walks away from the conversation, do not hesitate to tell him, and remind him that communication is between two. It's not easy to keep Gemini's interest, in fact, he doesn't know how to stay focused. This sign has practically seen it all and the best way to keep his gaze fixed is to keep him on his toes.

Make the necessary changes, and don't forget to never compromise your values or needs. As you get to know Gemini, have fun discovering your own multi-diversity. The seduction technique that works with Gemini is to talk, and being the most multi-faceted sign, they will love to tell you about their hobbies and interests.

Because it is so curious, conversing with this sign is like looking into a mirror, as it has the wonderful ability to reflect whatever you say to it. This may seem like a strange thing to say, but it's really the nature of this sign. Dating a Gemini is an exhilarating experience, you must be careful because Gemini requires constant stimulation, which sometimes makes it difficult to get to know them on a deep emotional level. Be sure to make time to sit and chat with your Gemini partner without distractions, and don't be afraid to remind him or her that pleasant receptions are never wasted time.

Gemini loves sex, for him it is another form of communication. Gemini possesses a strong sexual appetite, and to turn him on, all it takes is a couple of insightful comments. When it comes to dirty talk, Gemini wrote an encyclopedia, so you can turn him on by explaining exactly what you like to do in bed. This way he will feel and analyze at the same time, a combination that he is orgasmic.

One of the peculiarities of Gemini is the speed with which he can recover from the most devastating mistakes. Unlike other signs, he is not ruled by his ego. He likes to have fun, so he doesn't let his ego get in his way, so when he makes a mistake, he never gets defensive.

If Gemini has to offer an apology they will do so immediately. Although this quality is super respected, it is not completely generous. Gemini expects you to accept their apology with equal haste.

Gemini is happiest when he is busy; as soon as his schedule becomes too relaxed, he finds a way to change things up. It's not that he's afraid of it, it's just that he doesn't like to be bored.

All of this can be a challenge for Gemini couples. Stable relationships require a lot of nurturing, and Gemini can't offer that easily, so when you're in a partnership, you need to make sure you're prioritizing your relationships.

As this air sign is willing to try everything at least once, but sometimes twice, they enjoy exploring various aspects of their personality through their romantic relationships.

Although he does not project it, Gemini is looking for a serene partner to balance his intimate or family space, since for modifications he already has enough of his own. This air sign is constantly looking for someone with whom it can maintain a good relationship, and for that reason it is always wandering.

Gemini and Aries are a strong relationship with all kinds of dynamics including friendship and romance. Both Aries and Gemini enjoy their mistakes and appreciate each other's momentum. With their jokes, code words and fun, Gemini and Aries bring out the best in each other.
The danger, however, is that neither Gemini nor Aries are particularly good at calling it a night.
In this pairing, it is important for one to take responsibility. Otherwise, it may be difficult for these party lovers to cultivate a healthy and emotionally sound relationship.

Gemini and Taurus are not a comfortable relationship, but if both are committed, they can *achieve a lasting relationship. Taurus, with his strong character, is never afraid to set boundaries. Gemini has a completely different way of looking at the world, so he doesn't understand Taurus' avid demand for security. However, if they can negotiate between permanence and transience, they can teach each other invaluable lessons.*

If Taurus and Gemini are willing to make substantial changes to compensate for each other's needs, this relationship has the potential to be challenging and entertaining.

Two Gemini, *it's like a party in the middle of the day. They understand each other deeply, and never tire of it. The problem with this couple is that they can lack perspective.*

For a Gemini² relationship to be successful in the long run, each must be sure to learn to listen. Both of you will have many innovative ideas, but unless one of you is willing to offer stability, you run the risk of losing control and killing the relationship.

Gemini and Cancer *can build a beautiful relationship if they want to. Cancer has a very characteristic approach to life because it is very sensitive and intuitive, and needs a lot of love, and validation to feel secure.*

At first, it may seem that the cerebral Gemini could never offer that kind of configuration, but Gemini is flexible. If Cancer knows how to communicate its needs directly, Gemini will go out of its way to meet your requirements.

Cancer's deep emotions and sensitivity are also challenged by Gemini's detachment. However, if Gemini takes off the mask, this can be a partner worth keeping.

Ultimately, although this relationship requires some effort and investment, these signs can build a compassionate and fun connection.

Gemini and Leo are the spirit of any party, together they form an effective and active couple to be noticed and listened to. Leo is seduced by being the center of the action, and nothing seduces Gemini more than finding celebration.

These two social ambassadors are happy in meetings but differ on many points.
Leo loves to shine in front of the public, but in the end what he is looking for is an honest relationship.

Gemini, on the other hand, is not interested in impressing anyone. In fact, Gemini is all about feeding their avid curiosity. When Leo wants to establish trust, Gemini wants to have fun.

As a result, Leo may appreciate Gemini as insensitive, while Gemini may be frustrated by Leo's needs.

However, through communication, they can learn to have a relationship based on searching and having fun.

Gemini and Virgo, *ruled by Mercury, the planet of communication, share a sublime understanding and appreciation for expression. However, despite this influence, these two signs have very different ways of conveying information. Gemini is all about evasiveness, while Virgo is eminently accessible.*

Gemini is insightful and quick with their thoughts, while Virgo, an astute analyst and processor, prefers ideas only after properly organizing them. As a result, a relationship between these two signs requires them to work hard to make sure they share and listen to each other equally.

Otherwise, Gemini is likely to end up monopolizing the conversation, while Virgo stores up a taciturn anger towards his exorbitantly chatty comrade.

Gemini, being sociable, can also make Virgo frantic or jealous, however, when each sign lets their guard down and decides to have fun, this relationship has potential.

There is an instant connection between ***Gemini and Libra*** *when they are paired together. The two align in perfect balance. The two of them share fun talks,* charming stories, and many fabulous festivities. However, tension can arise when Libra, with all its glamour, feels let down by Gemini's teasing.

The truth is that Gemini talks about everything to everything with anyone, and Libra, is more selective when it comes to initiating a conversation, something Gemini may find a bit presumptuous. However, if each sign can abide by the other's approach, the couple can last a long time.

Gemini and Scorpio are easily unbalanced. Gemini is too busy with life's many emotions to get caught up in a specific drama, while Scorpio would never dare let his guard down unless he knew it was a reality.

Interestingly, Gemini and Scorpio are attracted to each other in a powerful and seductive way. Gemini is mesmerized by Scorpio's spirituality, and Scorpio is preoccupied with trying to win Gemini's affection.

At first, the relationship is stimulated by desire, but once the couple is instituted, they must face some major difficulties. The resourceful Gemini needs freedom, while the powerful Scorpio demands unwavering loyalty.

And while Gemini is flexible, Scorpio clings to their feelings, so it's important for both of you to practice reading each other's modalities. This couple is not *easy, but they have extraordinary chemistry, especially sexual, and this can make this relationship worth all the work.*

Gemini and Sagittarius *are compatible, in fact, this couple is one of the most dynamic in the entire zodiac. These signs are wanderers by nature and when they come together, they form an incredibly primal recreation-loving power couple.*

They have similar approaches to life and approach the world with the same frenzy and optimism. Gemini and Sagittarius are natural storytellers, and the mental stimulation between these two signs causes neurons to project at high speed.

Basically, this is a relationship that does not require a lot of work, but you should not take your relationship for granted. Every relationship requires trust and commitment, so both of you should make sure you don't take too many liberties.

Circumstantially, the ego of Sagittarius can cause problems, but Gemini with his skills of suggestion will know how to channel the circumstances. Obviously, Sagittarius has a lot to boast about, but he should be humbler.

Gemini and Capricorn, *it is a relationship that takes a lot of dedication. Capricorn gawks at Gemini. The* *hardest working sign of the zodiac doesn't understand how someone so erratic can achieve so much success. While Capricorn wears himself out working, Gemini, like a sorcerer shows the varied ways in which he achieves success, leaving Capricorn amazed and completely smitten.*

Through communication, these two can gradually learn to understand each other better. To build a healthy relationship, Capricorn must allow Gemini to change its mind frequently.

Gemini must communicate their thought process to Capricorn, so that their earthy partner can reason out the reasons for their disproportionate changes of heart. Ultimately, the dynamics of this relationship can work, but it will require consecration on both sides.

Gemini and Aquarius *are like-minded. Aquarius is very intrigued by the insightful Gemini, and the Gemini, in turn, is enchanted by Aquarius' unchanging attitude and deeply humane passion.*

Gemini and Aquarius understand each other maturely and know how to sharpen each other's imagination with great dialogue. However, Aquarius is known for its extreme rebellious ideas, which, while wonderful, can annoy Gemini, who tends to prefer familiarity to rebelliousness. However, despite a small ellipsis of instruction, it is easy for these two to learn to be together. This relationship can develop into a formal and lasting romance over time.

Gemini and Pisces *have a complex relationship. As Gemini is personified by twins, this air sign wears its duality on its face. For its part, Pisces' multiple profiles are less visible to the naked eye.*

 The sign of Pisces represents two united fish moving in opposite directions, symbolizing their relationship to both the subtle and earthly realms.
As both are two-faced, they understand each other's need for freedom and research. However, neither Gemini nor Pisces is good at creating boundaries, so this couple must fight hard to create a dynamic.

Pisces is sensitive and may be suspicious of the purposes behind Gemini's sly subtlety. Meanwhile, Gemini is likely to think Pisces is overly dramatic. To function, this couple needs to communicate honestly and without games.

Money Rituals

Ritual to Increase Clientele
You need:

- 5 rue leaves

- 5 verbena leaves

- 5 rosemary leaves

- 5 grains of coarse sea salt

- 5 coffee beans

- 5 grains of wheat

- 1 magnet stone

- 1 white cloth bag

- Red thread

- Red ink

- 1 business card

- 1 pot with a large green plant

- 4 citrine quartz

Place all the materials inside the white bag, except for the magnet, the card, and the citrines. Next, sew it with red thread, then write the name of the business on the outside with red ink. For a full week leave the bag under the counter or in a drawer in your desk. After this time, you bury it in the bottom of the flowerpot next to the magnet stone and the business card. Finally, place the four citrines on top of the soil of the pot in the direction of the four cardinal points.

Ritual to Accelerate Sales.

This is an effective recipe for the protection of money, the multiplication of sales in your business and the energetic healing of the place.

You need:

-1 green candle

-1 coin

- sea salt

-1 pinch of hot pepper

You must perform this ritual on a Thursday or Sunday at the time of the planet Jupiter or the Sun. There should be no other people in the business premises.

Light the candle and around it, in the shape of a triangle, place the coin, a handful of salt and the pinch of hot pepper. It is essential that you place the pepper on the right and the handful of salt on the left. The coin should be at the top of the pyramid.

Stay for a few minutes in front of the candle and visualize everything you are wishing for regarding prosperity. The remains you can throw them away, the coin you keep in your place of business as protection.

Ritual to Attract Money with the Full Moon.
You need:

- *- 1 silver coin*

- *- 1 gold candle*

- *- 1 white quartz tip*

- *- Sea salt*

- *- Cup with Holy Water*

- *- 1 cinnamon incense*

- *- 1 metal tray*

On a small round table, you will place one ingredient from each element. The tray with sea salt representing the earth, a candle as a symbol of fire, the cup with sacred water representing water, and the incense representing air.

Raise each symbol towards the sky pointing to the cardinal point that represents it. Once this is done, light the candle.

Place the coin and the quartz tip in the cup with water, light the incense and pass the cup with the coin over the candle repeating: "Beautiful Moon, bring me prosperity, fill my hands with money".

Repeat five times.

When the candle is consumed, throw away the water and keep the coin and the quartz in a secret place where no one can touch it.

Prosperity Material

You need:

- 7 coins in common use, but of high value

- 7 bay leaves

- 1 deep fountain

- Coarse sea salt

Cook bay leaves in water until the water turns dark green.

Remove from heat and wait for it to cool sufficiently.

Then fill the bowl with sea salt, wash the coins in the laurel extract water and bury them in the sea salt.

Take out the bay leaves that you cooked and put them in the dish.

During this process you should ask for the increase of your prosperity, visualize it.

Store the bowl with the coins, salt, and bay leaves in an inaccessible place.

Material Abundance All Year Long.

You need:

- 1 cup full of sacred water

- 1 grape

- 1 low denomination banknote of current use

- Brown sugar

- 1 white handkerchief

Introduce the grape and the banknote into the cup filled with sacred water. Leave it exposed to the light of the Full Moon, if possible, in the open air.

For the next three nights after midnight add a teaspoon of brown sugar.

On the fourth day, dry the bill in the sun and once dry, wrap it in the white handkerchief. Keep the bill in an unused wallet or purse and bury the grape in a jar with soil.

To guarantee the success of this ritual, repeat it five times a year. The bills used should be kept inside the same handkerchief and the grapes should be buried.

Ritual for Luck in Gambling.

On a lottery ticket you write the amount of money you want to win on the front of the ticket and on the back your name. Burn the ticket with a green candle. Collect the ashes in a purple paper and bury them.

Make your Stone to Earn Money
You need:

- Earth

- Sacred Water

- 7 coins of any denomination

- 7 pyrite stones.

- 1 green candle

- 1 teaspoon cinnamon

- 1 teaspoon sea salt

- 1 teaspoon brown sugar

- 1 teaspoon rice

You must perform this ritual under the light of the full moon, i.e., outdoors.

Inside a container pour the water with the earth so that it becomes a thick mass. Add to the mixture the teaspoons of salt, sugar, rice and cinnamon, and place in different places, in the middle of the dough, the 7 coins and the 7 pyrites.

Evenly mix this mixture, smoothing it with a spoon.

Leave the container under the light of the full moon all night, and part of the next day in the sun to dry.

Once dry, take it inside your house and place the lit green candle on top of it. Do not clean this stone from the wax residues. Place it in your kitchen, as close to a window as possible.

Make Money with the Lunar Cup.

You need:

- 1 crystal glass

- 1 large plate

- Fine sand

- Gold glitter

- 4 cups sea salt

- 1 malachite quartz

- 1 cup of sea, river, or holy water

- Cinnamon sticks or cinnamon powder

- Dried or fresh basil

- Fresh or dried parsley

- Corn kernels

- 3 bills of current denomination

Place the three folded bills, cinnamon sticks, corn kernels, malachite, basil, and parsley inside the glass.

Mix the glitter with the sand and add it to the cup until it is filled.

Under the light of the Full Moon, place the plate with the four cups of sea salt.

Place the cup in the middle of the plate, surrounded by the salt.

Pour the cup of sacred water into the dish, so that it moistens the salt well, leave it all night in the light of the Full Moon, and part of the day until the water vaporizes and the salt is dry again.

Add four or five grains of salt to the glass and discard the rest.

Take the cup inside your home, somewhere visible or where you keep your money.

Every full moon day you will spread a little of the contents of the cup in every corner of your house and sweep it up the next day.

Spell to be a Millionaire.

You need:

- 3 pyrites or citrine quartz

- 3 gold coins

- 1 gold-colored candle

- 1 red sachet

On the first day of the Full Moon, you place a table near a window where you can observe the Full Moon; on the table you will place the coins and quartz in the shape of a triangle.

Light the candle, place it in the middle and looking at the Moon repeat three times the following prayer: "Full Moon that illuminates my life, use the power you have to attract me money and make these coins multiply".

When the candle is consumed, put the coins and quartz with the right hand in the red bag, carry it always with you, it will be your talisman to attract money, no one should touch it.

Ritual to Get a Job

You need:

- 1 green candle

- Peppermint leaves

- Sandalwood oil

- 1 tablespoon cinnamon powder

- 1 sewing needle

Write on the green candle with the needle "I wish to have an excellent job", then you must consecrate the candle with your hands by rubbing the sandalwood oil and sprinkling the cinnamon.

Light the candle and place the peppermint leaves around it. When the candle burns out you can throw everything in the trash.

Ritual for People who are going to work for the first time.

This ritual is performed with the New Moon or Crescent Quarter at the time of the planet Mars or Mercury.

You place seven yellow candles around your photo. Burn a sandalwood incense during this ritual. Take some parsley and place it around the photo.

Concentrate intensely on the fundamental objective (getting a job). Then light the yellow candles in a counterclockwise direction.

You pronounce the following prayer, three times in a row: "My Guardian Angel grant me the job of (say the profession you want to get)". The remains of the candles and the photo should be buried.

Spell to Improve your Financial Income.

You need:

- 1 yellow handkerchief

- 1 gold candle

- 4 gold coins

- 1 white porcelain vessel

- 4 tablespoons of honey

- 1 yellow rose

- 1 small octagonal piece of paper

- black ink

- 1 metal cauldron

Place the metal cauldron on top of the yellow handkerchief, insert the golden candle with the four coins inserted in line and the container with the honey. On top of the honey, you put the yellow rose.

Write with black ink your petition on the paper and insert it in a ball. Light the candle for half an hour in the morning and at night, while you repeat out loud the petition you wrote on the paper.

After half an hour you must cover everything that is in the handkerchief. After nine days, take the remains of the candle, the container with the honey and the flower, wrap it all with the mat and close it with seven knots.

You must throw the package on your back, with your right hand and eyes closed, into the sea or into a river of moving waters at the time of the planet Venus.

Money Magnet

You need:

- 1 empty wine glass

- 2 green candles

- 1 handful of white rice

- 12 legal tender coins

- 1 magnet

- White rice

You light the two candles that should be located one on each side of the wine glass. At the bottom of the glass, you put the magnet.

Then you take a handful of white rice and place it in the cup. Then place the twelve coins inside the cup.

When the candles are consumed to the end, place the coins in the prosperity corner of your home or business.

Best Countries and Cities to Live In

Countries: *United States, Belgium, Iceland, Tunisia, Armenia, Wales.*

Cities: *Egypt, Brabant, Flanders. Lombardy, Tripoli, Bruges, London.*

Incense and Essential Oils for Money

Cinnamon incense for its ability to attract positive vibrations, peace, prosperity, protection, money, and happiness.

Plants for Money

Jasmine. *You don't need any gardening knowledge to grow it. And it is one of the plants that attract money and prosperity.*

Lavender: *this plant is used as a main element in rituals, to attract money and get rid of bad omens.*

Quartz for Money

Carnelian: *A Quartz widely used by the Egyptians and Romans to overcome obstacles. It protects from material goods.*

Gemini and Vocation

Gemini has excellent mental agility and is very curious. It is a sign that knows how to take advantage of opportunities to increase its knowledge.

His ability to communicate, and mastery of multiple subjects, synchronize to allow him to relate with ease in the areas he frequents.

Monotony does not suit this sign. They have a need for intellectual stimulation and to persistently expand their knowledge in various areas of interest. The impatient nature of Gemini requires constant change. Otherwise, their spirit is discouraged and destroyed.

Best Professions

Gemini are multifaceted people. They are the most affable, friendly, and communicative sign of the zodiac. They are best suited to careers that interact with the public and offer variety. They are very versatile, so they are prone to change careers many times. Journalism, media in general, musical, or theatrical performers, public relations, writers, and sales.

Vacations

Vacations provide physical and mental benefits. It has been proven that vacationing lowers stress levels and benefits the immune system. Sometimes planning a vacation causes stress because there are infinite options and deciding becomes a chimerical task.

Using astrology, understanding your personality provides insight into the ideal vacation spot for you.

***Aries**, an all-inclusive resort with outdoor sports activities in a warm location like Punta Cana, Cancun and the Turks and Caicos Islands would be ideal. Australia is an exciting country that offers a wealth of emotions to make your heart race.*

***Taurus**, a stay in a luxurious resort on Cayman Island, or a luxurious vacation in Dubai, in a hotel that has all the amenities will be very appealing. Italy is a perfect country because there you will find everything you have always dreamed of love, charm, luxury, wonderful food, and first-class wines.*

***Gemini** loves to feel intellectually engaged. Travel with guided excursions such as a safari in Africa or researching the species of the Galapagos Islands offer the zodiac communicator a luxurious experience.*

Cancer, short trips, surrounded by family and friends. Disney World, enjoying the attractions and its diverse foods is one option. In Orlando, Florida, there are multiple fantastic hotels and resorts, each with a unique and fascinating theme.

Leo, staying in a bungalow over the sea in Tahiti is fantastic for this sign. Another luxury alternative, something the lion loves, would be to rent a private tropical island in the Maldives, Fiji, or the Virgin Islands.

Virgo, Italy is your best option. This country will keep you well occupied. As an earth sign you connect with the world around you, places like La Romana in the Dominican Republic, Puerto Viejo in Costa Rica, and Belo Horizonte in Brazil will inject life into you.

Libra, go for cities with museums. Tropical vacations will not be as satisfying for Libra as touring the Louvre in Paris, the Acropolis Museum in Athens, Greece, the Prado Museum in Madrid, Spain or the Uffizi Gallery in Florence, Italy.

Scorpion, spend a few days on a secluded beach with liquor and massages. In Greece, Bali, St. Martin, or Hawaii you will find all these luxuries. Visiting heritage sites near your luxury hotel would be an extraordinary combination of tropical and cultural vacation. Mykonos and Roda in Greece are perfect destinations.

Sagittarius, explore the Camino de Santiago, a network of very different paths, all leading to the city of Santiago de Compostela. Each path has its history, heritage, and magic. Sagittarius is a traveler who craves new experiences so in Ireland you will find everything you are looking for.

Capricorn, a goal-oriented sign. Vacations where you can make new business relationships. China would be spectacular. Capricorn has a sense of historical value that other signs do not have, so countries like Israel and Egypt where history is present will make you feel at home.

Aquarius loves new ideas, unknown places, and new relationships. A fantastic country to visit would be Japan not only for its fascinating history and culture, but because each of its regions has something different to offer.

Pisces*, a water sign that is happy with tropical vacations. A beachfront hotel would be ideal. The island "La Dique" in the Republic of Seychelles, perhaps the most beautiful beach in the world will be a sure success. Pisces, possessing a calm outlook on life, being ruled by Neptune makes you a creative thinker. Sweden is a country he should visit because there he will find a culture as innovative as he is.*

Who is your soul mate according to your zodiac sign?

When we hear the term "soul mates," we usually think of them as referring to members of a couple, i.e., someone with whom you have a strong sentimental-sexual connection. However, legitimate soul mates do not always relate to each other from that point of view, and often are not even interested in the sexual aspect of a relationship.

Your soul mate may not only be your partner, but also your parent, friend, child, grandparent, boss, or sister.

From the astrological point of view and considering that the lessons we need to learn before reaching the next spiritual level are the ones that define the type of affective relationships, we need to develop in life today, we can say that Cancer and Pisces are soul mates of Aries.

With Cancer and Pisces, Aries can not only focus better and resolve conflicts without violence, but also develop empathy, that is, the ability to put themselves in the other's place and learn to share.

These two signs do not like conflicts, and if they do arise, they prefer dialogue to any episode of brutality.

Aries can teach Cancer and Pisces not to need the approval of others, to be more risk-taking, and not to try to please everyone, i.e., to be more assertive.

The sensual Taurus, enemy of change, inbred relative of inertia, has as his soul mate Sagittarius and Gemini, two signs that know that life is a fascinating journey, but not a static one.

They can teach Taurus that it does not have to stay where it no longer must be for fear of uncertainty, and that there will always be certain situations or circumstances that will happen without us expecting them, and without us possessing any power to modify them. Taurus also has a lot to teach these signs.

Lessons of willpower, to have commitments with others, to be committed to what they do and to continue to the end with persistence, without haste or slowness. To have principles, and to be prudent.

Leo can balance a lot of karma with their soul mates belonging to Libra and Aquarius.

A Leo may become obstinate with a wrong idea or belief out of vanity; Libra and Aquarius know that behind an egocentric person there is a low self-esteem.

Libra will teach Leo equanimity and tolerance, to use reasoning and diplomacy to maintain smooth communication. Aquarius, the opposite sign to Leo, equipped with objective and fair judgment as they are never swayed by prejudice, will teach Leo to see people's hearts, to offer their shoulder and give sympathetic words in times of need.

Leo never hesitates when making decisions, and if they do, they do not manifest it, something that Libra should practice.

Fidelity is a hallmark in Leo, something unknown to Aquarius, and the little lions can give him moral lessons.

Virgo, known as perfectionists because of their immense fear of failure, has Scorpio and Capricorn as soul mates. Virgo likes to be rigorous in their decisions and has a prototype in almost every aspect of their life. This selectivity holds them back from following the movement of life.

Virgo will literally tear an entire project apart if they feel it wasn't perfect in the first place, something a Capricorn would never do as their vision will allow them to see that alternative measures can always be taken, without having to start over.

Capricorn is a sign sure of their own space, they don't make meaningless decisions, something Virgo sometimes does.

On the other hand, Scorpio can mitigate the worst and enhance the best of Virgo. Scorpio and Virgo have a practical approach to life; however, Scorpio is much more of a life-lover than Virgo. Scorpio will bring the decisiveness that Virgo lacks, and Virgo will bring control and rationality to the passionate Scorpio.

Virgo will make Capricorn more pleasant and playful at his side, isolating him from that excessive seriousness that he often shows in his face.

Madness and the Signs of the Zodiac.

Madness has been revealed throughout history as an obscure, enigmatic, and conflicting truth. It has frightened us, we have ignored it and even accepted it, and as a result, the people who have supposedly suffered from it have been rejected, eliminated, and honored.

Any behavior that is incongruent with our reasoning is not necessarily an act of insanity, but a different way of proceeding.

It is a mistake if, when we feel affected or annoyed by the actions or follies of others, we banish them, since this does not make us more reasonable, balanced, or perfect, but rather makes us just as crazy.

Defining insanity is as complex as defining sanity, but all zodiac signs have their degree of insanity.

Cancer: They are temperamental. This causes them to have an incomprehensible personality seen from the outside. The popularity of crazy people was earned by their inconsistent character that sometimes disturbs the people around them.

Scorpio: They need change to be happy, they can do crazy things just to generate some action. For them having an outburst is normal because they are addicted to change and frenzies.

Pisces: *It is impossible for them not to infect you with their madness. Their instability and imbalance bother the people around them. They see everything as rosy, which makes them be called crazy because they are always floating on a cloud.*

Gemini: *He is famous for his duality. They are sometimes in conflict with themselves. They love challenges that involve danger. They love to plan impromptu adventures and are always ready to border the limits of maximum madness.*

Leo: *When the fire settles in their head, they think that everything that surrounds their life is more urgent than anything else. They are extravagant and have attitudes that for others are considered crazy. They can do things that a reasonable person would never do.*

Aries: *They upset themselves and anyone around them. They are stubborn and like to be the first in everything, even if for that they must commit crazy* *things. They do not know how to take it back, something that leads them to perform irrational acts.*

Aquarius: *A rebellious and free sign, which does not care in the least about the opinion they have of them. It acts in a capricious way, with crazy attitudes that break the paradigms.*

Sagittarius: *He is fun, but violent with his desire for action. They do not know how to measure the consequences of their actions, something that many consider madness. It is not strange to see them totally unbridled, crossing the terrain of irresponsibility.*

Libra: *They long for happiness and harmony, and to get it they are willing to do anything crazy. They are unstable, and that leads them to break their commitments, something that many consider crazy.*

Virgo: *They go to extremes and become obsessive. They have a vision of what they want written in stone, no one can give them advice, they do not let themselves be guided. When they do not listen, they commit various follies.*

Taurus: *When an idea lands in their mind there is no one to banish it, even committing crazy things to corroborate their hypothesis. Try to test their patience and you will discover how far their level of madness goes.*

Capricorn: *He forgets absolutely nothing, does not forgive and much less, forgets, if you do something wrong, do not worry because he will remind you for a lifetime to drive you completely crazy. Capricorn is insanely obsessive about control.*

The psychology behind the lottery.

Lottery games are very popular all over the world.

We all have the impossible dream of winning the lottery, since the illusion of being millionaires, by a stroke of luck, even if the odds are minimal, is the main reason why people play.

Players perceive that the cost of the lottery ticket, in relation to the profits they would obtain if they won, is minuscule. We always perceive risk emotionally, and if it causes us pleasure, we tend to see the risk as insignificant and neutralize the emotion of danger, focusing only on the benefits.

Players see the lottery as a unique opportunity to be rewarded by investing little money, and with little exposure to risk.

Games have both traditional and superstitious aspects. Some people always play the same numbers because they are their favorites, relate them to a significant date, or have dreamed them.

Others play at a specific time, day, or place. When we think we are in control, we feel confident, because when we choose the numbers ourselves, instead of playing at random, although the chances of being right are the same, we have the impression that we are controlling destiny, and that the chances are in our favor.

There are people who only play for fun, in these cases the lottery transcends the economic cost, becoming a fun that is enlivened when they conjecture everything, they can do with the money they would acquire.

There are five psychological descriptions of individual lottery players:

The adventurer, *who is bewitched by games involving large sums of money, speculating with random numbers, and with planned numbers.*

The competitor, *who insists on showing off through gambling that he bets to win.*

The greedy, *who has no boundaries for gambling, and is not afraid to take risks when betting.*

The tactician, *never playing risky, looks for tactics, strategies, and numerical sets when playing the numbers.*

The superstitious person, *who always plays the same number combinations, uses talismans, rituals, or will buy his tickets on a specific date and place.*

Is there a trick or formula to win the lottery?

That question is still unanswered. There are many who speculate, and claim, that you are more likely to be struck by lightning before you win the lottery. Although others study the odds with great perseverance and subtlety.

Playing the lottery, or any other game of chance if it is done with measure, is a cheap way to buy illusions and confidence in the future. The complication arises when the person does not control his impulses to play, generating an addiction to gambling and falling into compulsive gambling.

A gambling addict is an individual to whom gambling causes great difficulties at work and in his family relationships, since losses induce him to gamble larger amounts of money with the aspiration of recovering the lost money. This becomes a vicious circle, and the only way to solve it is with psychotherapeutic treatment.

The best gift for zodiac signs this Christmas.

Gift giving is a universal way to show that we care and appreciate a person, but gift buying can be a challenge, for some a real headache.

The planets can help you once, knowing the zodiac sign of the person, you may be able to make the ideal gift.

Fire signs: Aries, Leo and Sagittarius *like gifts that make them feel important, related to sports, travel, and technology.*

A professional digital camera, the latest model of iPhone, a plane ticket with hotel included to an exotic tourist spot or with historical background, business books, sportswear or exercise equipment, lottery tickets, bottles of fine wine and exclusive branded shoes will please these signs greatly.

Taurus, Virgo and Capricorn*, who belong to the earth element, are sometimes traditional, but that doesn't mean they don't like gifts from recognized brands.*

A painting of a famous painter, a belt or briefcase to carry their work papers, a wallet with their initials, branded perfumes, massages or body treatments, a pet, bathrobes, cozy pajamas, or even aromatherapy diffusers will make them happy.

Air signs: Gemini, Libra and Aquarius are not materialistic, and the functionality of a gift is much more important than the price. Their imagination is abundant, and anything that stimulates this capacity appeals to them.

A cell phone, computer or iPad, books on personal growth, spirituality, philosophy and alternative therapies, self-help and economic empowerment courses, a telescope, tickets to the opera or theater, an animal that does not have to be caged, quartz, essential oils, incense, and after-bath colognes will be highly appreciated by these signs.

Cancer, Scorpio and Pisces, the water signs, will love personalized gifts. Cooking utensils, a romantic dinner on the beach under the moonlight, a relaxing massage in a spa, daring lingerie, slippers or a comfortable sofa to watch TV, a bottle of champagne, scented candles, amulets, astrology books, a set of tarot cards, lotions, perfumes and beauty accessories, wine, cookies, preserves and all variety of gourmet products are on the list of gifts that these signs will accept with great pleasure.

Giving gifts is a blessing, it is a gesture of generosity; giving gifts is a symbolic act that represents a compliment, an attention to someone we want to please and symbolizes the affection we profess.

When we give gifts, relationships are improved and strengthened, and joy is generated.

The zodiac signs and their fears.

The twelve signs of the zodiac symbolize twelve essential archetypes of the human personality, but at the same time they are psychological prototypes, which is why each of the zodiac signs has a very specific and personal fear.

Let us remember that fear is an essential human alarm and defense mechanism. It only becomes a problem when it is excessive.

*Fears are insecurities and sometimes we project them with the opposite actions as it is the case of the **Aries** sign; recognized for their iron will, nothing and nobody paralyzes them. They love to control everything, and their most ingrained fear is to fail or ask for help, because for them this is synonymous of weakness.*

***Taurus** is the most stubborn of the earth signs. Change terrifies them, as well as running out of money, they spend their lives saving because poverty frightens them.*

***Gemini**, the communicator of the zodiac, a bit anxious and insecure, they try to attract attention because they dread looking boring. Legitimate children of the*

Moon, Cancers love their safety zone because no one can hurt them there, they are terrified of loneliness and rejection.

Leo, the king of the zodiac, leaders and brave, were not born to lose. Their most ingrained fear is to go unnoticed; they prefer to be spoken ill of, but not to be ignored.

The master of neatness **Virgo** sometimes becomes compulsive about health, so they are hypochondriacs. Their main fear is getting sick, but disorganization scares them more than anything else.

Exceptionally intelligent **Librans** are indecisive and therein lies their primary fear: making decisions. Another of their fears is loneliness.

The enigmatic and seductive **Scorpios** have an elephant's memory, they fear betrayal and if you do something they dislike, they will keep it from you forever. Never keep a secret from a Scorpio.

The adventurer of the zodiac, **Sagittarius is** terrified of commitment because the demands are terrifying. They *are very funny, but behind that smile hides the fear of being deceived.*

*Demanding to the extreme, **Capricorns** never stray from their goals; their main fear is to make mistakes, especially at the professional level. They are self-sacrificing and fear not achieving their dreams.*

*The rebellious and utopian **Aquarius** fear losing their freedom, this would mean losing their own essence. They always have many friendships, but none of them bind them. They need the group, but do not want the group to need them.*

*Peace is synonymous with **Pisces**, they hate confrontations. Compassionate to the core, they are afraid to see others suffer. They are a little insecure, have stage fright and fear rejection.*

Some old astrology books hold Saturn totally responsible for fear in a natal chart, I think that for fear to originate, the alliance of several planets with their corresponding energies must manifest.

That is, fears are represented by several planets linked by aspects, there is no specific planet that is necessarily related to the development of any type of fear.

Moon in Gemini

The Moon is not comfortable in the sign of Gemini. Air signs don't know how to deal with intense emotions, and Gemini specifically moves so fast that maintaining deep emotions is very difficult for them.

The Moon in Gemini usually expresses itself with small flashes accompanied by sudden mood changes.

Gemini prefers to act in the social and mental area.

The Moon in Gemini wants to be free to explore duality and experience the full range of emotions, moving freely between opposite extremes of a situation.

If your Moon is in the sign of Gemini, you will feel more confident when you explore novel ideas and enjoy interacting socially with others.

Gemini is a sign that functions best operating on the surface as it is not interested in delving into the emotional world.

If your Moon is in Gemini, your comfort zone relates to keeping a range of options open. You need to feel that you are free to create your own opinion about different situations. You will always feel more comfortable when you can concentrate on more abstract and intellectual matters.

Words and language are specifically more important to you. All your safety concerns involve how you communicate in any situation with yourself.

The importance of the Ascendant Sign

The sun sign has a major impact on who we are, but the ascendant is what really defines us, and that could even be the reason why you don't identify with some traits of your zodiac sign.

Really the energy that your sun sign gives you makes you feel different from the rest of the people, for that reason, when you read your horoscope sometimes you feel identified and gives sense to some predictions, and that happens because it helps you to understand how you could feel and what will happen to you, but it only shows you a percentage of what could really be.

The ascendant on the other hand differs from the sun sign because it reflects who we are superficially, that is, how others see you or the energy you transmit to people, and this is so real that it may be the case that you meet someone and if you predict their sign you may have discovered their ascendant sign and not their sun sign.

In summary, the characteristics you see in someone when you first meet them is the Ascendant, but since our lives are affected by the way we relate to others, the Ascendant has a major impact on our daily lives.

It is a bit complex to explain how the rising sign is calculated or determined, because it is not the position of a planet that determines it, but the sign that was rising on the eastern horizon at the time of your birth, as opposed to your sun sign, which depends on the precise time you were born.

Thanks to technology and the Universe today is easier than ever to know this information, of course if you know your birth time, or if you have an idea of the time but there is not a margin of more than hours, because there are many websites that make the calculation by entering the data, astro.com is one of them, but there is infinite.

This way, when you read your horoscope you can also read your ascendant and know more personalized details, you will see that from now on if you do this your way of reading the horoscope will change and you will know why that Sagittarius is so modest and pessimistic if in fact they are so exaggerated and optimistic, and this is perhaps because he has a Capricorn Ascendant, or because that Scorpio colleague is always talking about everything, no doubt he has a Gemini Ascendant.

I am going to synthesize the characteristics of the different Ascendants, but this is also very general since these characteristics are modified by planets in conjunction with the Ascendant, planets aspecting the Ascendant, and the position of the sign's ruling planet on the Ascendant.

For example, a person with an Aries Ascendant with its ruling planet, Mars, in Sagittarius will respond to the environment a little differently than another person, also with an Aries Ascendant, but whose Mars is in Scorpio.

Similarly, a person with a Pisces Ascendant who has Saturn conjunct him will "behave" differently than someone with a Pisces Ascendant who does not have that aspect.

All these factors modify the Ascendant, astrology is very complex, and horoscopes are not read or made with tarot cards, because astrology is not only an art but also a science.

It can be common to confuse these two practices, and this is because, although they are two totally different concepts, they have some points in common. One of these common points is based on their origin and is that both procedures have been known since ancient times.

They are also similar in the symbols they use, since both present ambiguous symbols that need to be interpreted, requiring specialized reading and training to know how to interpret these symbols.

There are thousands of differences, but one of the main ones is that while in tarot the symbols are perfectly understandable at first glance, being figurative cards, although it is necessary to know how to interpret them well, in astrology we observe an abstract system which is necessary to know previously to interpret them, and of course it must be said that, although we can recognize the tarot cards, anyone can not interpret them correctly.

Interpretation is also a difference between the two disciplines because while tarot does not have an exact time reference, since the cards are placed in time only thanks to the questions asked in the corresponding spread, astrology does refer to a specific position of the planets in history, and the interpretation systems used by both are diametrically opposed.

The astrological chart is the basis of astrology, and the most important aspect to make the prediction. The astrological chart must be perfectly elaborated for the reading to be successful and to learn more about the person.

To draw up a birth chart, it is necessary to know all the data about the birth of the person in question.

It must be known exactly, from the exact time it was delivered, to the place where it was done.

The position of the planets at the time of birth will reveal to the astrologer the points he needs to draw up the birth chart.

Astrology is not only about knowing your future, but also about knowing the important points of your existence, both present and past, to make better decisions to decide your future.

Astrology will help you to know yourself better, so that you can change the things that block you or enhance your qualities.

And if the astrological chart is the basis of astrology, the tarot reading is fundamental in the latter discipline. Like who makes you the astrological chart, the seer who makes you the tarot spread, will be the key to the success of your reading, so it is best to ask for tarot readers recommended, and although surely you cannot answer specifically to all the questions you ask yourself in your life, a correct reading of the tarot spread, and the cards that come out in the roll, will help guide you about the decisions you make in your life.

In summary, astrology, and tarot use symbolism, but the main question is how all this symbolism is interpreted.

truly a person who masters both techniques will undoubtedly be a great help to the people who will ask for advice.

Many astrologers combine both disciplines, and regular practice has taught me that both usually flow very well, providing an enriching component in all prediction issues, but they are not the same and you cannot do a horoscope with tarot cards, nor can you do a tarot reading with an astrological chart.

Ascendant in Gemini

If you have an Ascendant in Gemini, you face life with curiosity for everything around you.

You possess a lot of versatility, and for that reason you have no difficulty adapting to any situation.

Sometimes you lose your focus easily as you become interested in too many things at once, and sometimes you don't get a firm grasp on any of them.

The partner is very important for you, if you have the Ascendant in Gemini, as you fear getting lost in your mental ocean and you need someone to help you out of that labyrinth.

You always try to show a cheerful, charismatic, and sociable personality. You have a charming charisma and that is why you find it easy to win people over.

Sometimes you can have absurd attitudes, this is because you are interested in too many things at the same time, and this can be reflected in your attitude towards your surroundings.

People with an Ascendant in Gemini can think one thing and a few hours later think the opposite, but this instability is part of their charm.

Aries - Gemini Ascendant

These people are very expressive, the initiative of Aries is combined with the curiosity of Gemini. These individuals like to be always exchanging ideas.

In the sentimental area, they find it very easy to establish intimacy with their partners, but sometimes they can destabilize their partner because they are very unstable.

At work they are innovative people with a lot of initiative. Their creativity and ease of adapting to everything is outstanding.

They may indulge in charlatanism, being prone to superficiality.

Taurus - Gemini Ascendant

Taurus with Gemini Ascendant are sensitive people.

In the work environment they have intuition for business and opportunities, they know how to keep secrets and interact when appropriate.

In their romantic relationships they are pleasant people, they know how to handle difficult situations, but they value their space very much, and this is a basic requirement for their relationships to work.

This ascendant tends to isolation, especially if they go through a difficult time, such as a breakup.

Gemini - Gemini Ascendant

Gemini with Gemini Ascendant is a person who has reinforced the characteristics of this sign. They are individuals with great mental agility and infinite curiosity.

They are masters in communication and assimilate any idea with ease, winning most of the discussions where they participate. They always have many friendships and relationships.

In the work area, they will do very well in a job related to communication. However, your instability may make it difficult for you to finish your projects.

In love relationships they are not serious people. They are seductive, but they do not have the constancy to maintain something formal.

Sometimes they speak without thinking, saying the first thing that crosses their mind and this causes many problems.

Cancer - Gemini Ascendant

Cancer with Gemini Ascendant are communicative, imaginative, and creative people.

They fall in love easily but are also soon disillusioned. This type of person is charming, but self-centered and capricious.

On the work front, they are devoted to work, have strong business skills, and are very persuasive.

Leo - Gemini Ascendant

Leo with Gemini Ascendant are sociable. Gemini's versatility allows Leo to be more flexible. They love to travel, to know new places, cultures, and thoughts.

At the work level, they reason very quickly and are persuasive, managing to present all their ideas with skill.

In their sentimental relationships they are professionals in the art of seduction. They love to attract attention and to be noticed. They are not very given to commitment since they need freedom and to experiment with multiple partners.

Virgo - Gemini Ascendant

This combination of signs is usually reserved and cherish their privacy and solitude.

In the work environment they love challenges, they are quite unstable, something that also manifests itself when it comes to starting a relationship.

They are more inclined to platonic love, i.e., a relationship that does not involve a commitment. To win them over you must appeal to their intellectual side.

These people are overly concerned about their family stability.

Libra - Gemini Ascendant

Libra with Gemini Ascendant are very extroverted and youthful people. At work they value everything that has to do with creativity.

In their sentimental relationships they like to share their life with someone they enjoy, they are very faithful and usually their relationships are long lasting since they are always in communication with their partner.

Some are prone to create false expectations when starting a relationship, which causes them to have many breakups.

Scorpio - Gemini Ascendant

Gemini Ascendant Scorpio is one of the most extraordinary minds. These people can achieve anything they set their minds to, because they know how and when to activate their potential.

In the workplace, they have leadership qualities, and excel in energy and efficiency. They are productive and this always pushes them to success.

In their sentimental relationships they are very rational, it is very difficult to decipher what they are thinking since they are people who do not like to expose their feelings.

If they set their minds to it, they can be romantic, although they are impulsive and impatient.

Sometimes they are manipulative and may abuse their authority.

Sagittarius - Gemini Ascendant

Sagittarius with Gemini Ascendant are outgoing and pleasant people. However, they can have an unstable personality, changing tastes quickly. They have a great sense of justice and carefully analyze any situation to always reach the most impartial verdict.

In the work environment, they are always successful in the field of communications and are mediators within their company.

They value their partner very much, however, he or she must provide intellectual stimulation and conversation, as they are people who love to talk.

Some have too many relationships and fail to settle down seriously with any of them.

Capricorn - Gemini Ascendant

Capricorn with Gemini Ascendant are people who have a great perception and a lot of responsibility.

In the work environment, they show great interest in everything they do.

They are successful in love because they concentrate their efforts to conquer the other person. However, they find it difficult to be attracted to someone.

Some of these people are ironic, which makes it difficult for them to relate.

Aquarius - Gemini Ascendant

Aquarius with Gemini Ascendant are idealistic and philosophical people. They are kind and enjoy their freedom very much.

In the professional area, they are receptive to any activity and stand out for their originality.

In the sentimental plane they have facility to begin any type of relationship. However, they will value friendship above love, and cannot bear to be confined in a relationship.

They are very eccentric and sometimes expose themselves to danger to assert their freedom.

Pisces - Gemini Ascendant

Pisces with Gemini Ascendant seeks professional fulfillment.

In the work environment they show an incredible capacity for everything, even synchronously.

In love, due to their instability, they are difficult to live with. This is a long-term difficulty. They are very susceptible to words.

Ed and Lorraine Warren. The Paranormal World and Astrology,

The paranormal investigations of Ed Warren, a demonologist, and Lorraine Warren, a clairvoyant, inspired the iconic horror film franchise "The Conjuring," which expanded to include the films Annabelle, The Nun, and The Curse of the Weeping Woman.

Lorraine Moran was born in Bridgeport on 01/21/1927 at 6:40 pm and began having clairvoyant experiences as a child. Her sign is Aquarius, a freedom-loving, independent-minded sign. Her Moon is in Capricorn, a responsible sign, which tries to carry the world on its shoulders.

Lorraine Warren's Virgo Ascendant conjunct Neptune in the 12th house is prominent and lets you know that the spirit world is familiar to her. The 12th house is associated with places of confinement, and Lorraine's work involved her selfless and spiritual assistance to families imprisoned in their homes with demons.

The ruler of your chart, Mercury, related to the Sun, further underscores your purpose in life through your work to free people from spiritual disruption through the media.

Ed Warren, born 07/09/1926, in Bridgeport, was a Navy veteran of World War II, and a former police officer. He later became a demonologist, and author. His sign is Virgo, psychologically his nature was nervous and his Moon, also in Virgo, made him prone to analyze his emotional reactions in detail.

Neptune dominates his chart. He was a person gifted with imagination, and psychic abilities. Ed was a mystic, like any Neptunian, who saw what few people can see.

This duo, before Hollywood turned their stories into blockbuster movies, made a name for themselves investigating paranormal occurrences. Both claimed to be qualified to investigate unusual phenomena. Lorraine could see auras around people since childhood, and Ed grew up in a haunted house, turning out to be a self-taught demonologist.

Lorraine and Ed Warren pooled their talents and investigated many paranormal cases. Among the creepiest is the case of the Annabelle doll which is kept in a locked glass box in the Warren's basement Hidden Museum.

A nurse received the doll as a gift and noticed that it began to change position. She and her roommate found parchment paper with messages written on it that read "Help me or help us." The doll began appearing in different rooms and leaking blood. They turned to a medium, who said the doll was being occupied by the spirit of a girl named Annabelle.

Ed and Lorraine became interested in the case, and after evaluating the doll, they concluded that the doll was not possessed, but manipulated by an inhuman presence. The Warren's assessment was that the spirit in the doll was seeking to possess a human host, as spirits do not possess inanimate objects.

The Warrens had high-profile cases, including the Perron family case that served as the inspiration for the movie The Conjuring.

In January 1971, this family moved to a farm in Rhode Island. The family began noticing strange occurrences that worsened over time. First it started with a missing broom, but things ended with angry spirits. When the Warrens were hired, they claimed the house was haunted by a spirit named Bathsheba, and interestingly a woman who had lived on the property in the 1800s was a Satanist suspected of being involved in a murder.

All the Warren's paranormal investigations were and remain intriguing, but the Amityville case brought them to fame.

In November 1974, Ronald DeFeo the oldest son of the DeFeo family, who was 23 years old, murdered his entire family in their beds with a .35 caliber rifle and this infamous case was the catalyst for the claim that spirits haunted the Amityville house.

In 1976, the Lutz family moved into the Long Island home and believed a demonic spirit was living with them. They claimed to see a slimy liquid seeping from the walls, a pig-like creature threatening them, and flying knives aimed directly at family members. They were only in the house for 28 days.

Ed and Lorraine Warren visited the house 20 days after the Lutzes left and sensed an overwhelming demonic presence. This story became so prominent that it spawned conspiracy theories, books, and movies, including the 1979 classic "The Amytiville Horror."

The Warrens conducted their paranormal investigations for free, making a living by selling books, movie rights, lectures, and tours of their museum. Ed Warren died of complications after a stroke on August 23, 2006. Lorraine Warren retired from investigations shortly thereafter but remained a consultant until her death in 2019 at the New England Paranormal Research Society a society that still exists.

About the Authors

In addition to her astrological knowledge, Alina Rubi has an abundant professional education; she holds certifications in Psychology, Hypnosis, Reiki, Bioenergetic Crystal Healing, Angelic Healing, Dream Interpretation and is a Spiritual Instructor. Rubi has knowledge of Gemology, which she uses to program stones or minerals and turn them into powerful Amulets or Talismans of protection.

Rubi has a practical and results-oriented character, which has allowed her to have a special and integrative vision of several worlds, facilitating solutions to specific problems. Alina writes the Monthly Horoscopes for the website of the American Association of Astrologers; you can read them at www.astrologers.com. At this moment she writes a weekly column in the newspaper El Nuevo Herald on spiritual topics, published every Sunday in digital form and on Mondays in print. He also has a program and weekly Horoscope on the YouTube channel of this newspaper. Her Astrological Yearbook is published every year in the newspaper "Diario las Américas", under the column Rubi Astrologa.

Rubi has written several articles on astrology for the monthly publication "Today's Astrologer", has taught classes on Astrology, Tarot, Palm Reading, Crystal Healing, and Esotericism. She has weekly videos on esoteric topics on her YouTube channel: Rubi Astrologa. She had her own Astrology show broadcasted daily through Flamingo T.V., has been interviewed by several T.V. and radio programs, and every year she publishes her "Astrological Yearbook" with the horoscope sign by sign, and other interesting mystical topics.

She is the author of the books "Rice and Beans for the Soul" Part I, II, and III, a compilation of esoteric articles, published in English, Spanish, French, Italian and Portuguese. "Money for All Pockets", "Love for All Hearts", "Health for All Bodies", Astrological Yearbook 2021, Horoscope 2022, Rituals and Spells for Success in 2022, Spells and Secrets, Astrology Classes, Rituals and Charms 2024 and Chinese Horoscope 2024 are all available in five languages: English, Italian, French, Japanese and German.

Rubi speaks English and Spanish perfectly, combining all her talents and knowledge in her readings. She currently resides in Miami, Florida.

*For more information you can visit **the website** www.esoterismomagia.com*

Alina A. Rubi is the daughter of Alina Rubi. She is currently studying psychology at Florida International University.

Since she was a child, she has been interested in all metaphysical and esoteric subjects and has practiced astrology and Kabbalah since she was four years old. She has knowledge of Tarot, Reiki, and Gemology. She is not only the author, but also the editor, along with her sister Angeline A. Rubi, of all the books published by her and her mother.

*For more information, please contact her by email: **rubiediciones29@gmail.com***

Made in the USA
Las Vegas, NV
07 May 2024

89667062R00066